CAROL PUGLIANO

EASY-TO-READ
FOLK
&

FAIRY TALE PLAYS

SCHOLASTIC
PROFESSIONAL **B**OOKS

NEW YORK • TORONTO • LONDON • AUCKLAND • SYDNEY

DEDICATION

To Mom and Dad,
for reading stories to me
over and over again.

Designed by Vincent Ceci and Jaime Lucero
Cover design by Vincent Ceci and Jaime Lucero
Cover illustration by Carolyn Croll
Interior illustrations by Carolyn Croll

ISBN: 0-590-93088-5
12 11 10 9 8 7 6 5 4 3 2   4 5/9

CONTENTS

INTRODUCTION

Why do children sit quietly, enchanted, when Cinderella and her prince dance their way to midnight? What makes them sigh with relief when Hansel and Gretel escape the witch, and cheer for the tortoise when he crosses the finish line? What is it about these stories from long ago that continues to capture children's imaginations, generation after generation? I think noted folk-literature scholar and author Bruno Bettelheim answered these questions well when he wrote, "Nothing can be as enriching and satisfying to child and adult alike as the folk fairy tale. More can be learned from them about the inner problems of human beings, and of the right solutions to their predicaments in any society, than from any other type of story within a child's comprehension."

Like Bettelheim, I believe that the rich storytelling of these classic tales far outweighs their shortcomings in terms of gender and cultural stereotyping. Nonetheless, in developing this play book, I tried to steer clear of tales that could be deemed controversial and to choose stories that possess universal themes—stories that are as applicable and appropriate today as they were when they were first created. My real driving force in selecting the tales was my own childhood. I chose the stories that have stayed with me ever since my parents read them to me when I was very young.

Your students may already be familiar with some or all of the tales in this book. Whether they are learning the tales for the first time or revisiting good friends, I hope that by reading and performing the plays, they will breathe new life into old favorites. Enjoy!

ABOUT THIS BOOK

Knowing that you have barely enough time to get through your required lesson plans, let alone opportunity to stage a play, I've organized this book in a manner that will make it easier for you to perform the plays and link them to your curriculum. The play's features are as follows:

✯ They are written in simple language and presented in easy-to-read type.
✯ They do not require elaborate sets or costumes.
✯ Although there may not be enough parts for every child in your class, the plays are short enough so that you can read or perform them several times, giving all students a chance to participate.

4

✛ Each play is followed by a Teaching Guide that is set up so you can easily extend the learning of the plays. The Teaching Guide includes:

- Background information about the story and its author.

- Questions to ask students before they read the play, both to gauge how much they already know about the subject matter and to start them thinking about the play's themes.

- A list of vocabulary words to review with kids before reading the play aloud.

- Questions to ask students after they read the play to check their comprehension.

- Tips on preparing your classroom for performing the play.

- Pre-performance warm-up exercises that tie in to the theme of the play. These exercises let children know that something different is about to happen and create a nice bridge between reading and performing.

- Cross-curricular extension activities, including math, language arts, science, and social studies, to extend the play's themes.

The Tortoise and the Hare

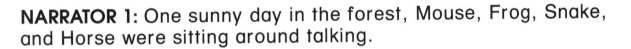

CHARACTERS

Narrator 1
Narrator 2
Hare
Mouse
Frog
Horse
Snake
Tortoise
Cheering Squad 1 (several students)
Cheering Squad 2 (remaining students)

NARRATOR 1: One sunny day in the forest, Mouse, Frog, Snake, and Horse were sitting around talking.

NARRATOR 2: All of a sudden, Hare ran up to them. He jogged in place as he spoke to the other animals.

HARE: I feel like running a race. Who would like to race with me? How about you, Mouse?

MOUSE: No, not me. I cannot scurry along fast enough to beat you!

HARE: You are right. How about you, Frog?

FROG: No, not me. I cannot hop along fast enough to beat you!

HARE: You are right. How about you, Horse?

HORSE: No, not me. I cannot gallop along fast enough to beat you!

HARE: You are right. How about you, Snake?

SNAKE: No, not me. I cannot sssssssslither along fast enough to beat you!

HARE: You are right. I am the fastest animal around! I have never been beaten in a race.

NARRATOR 1: At that moment, Tortoise appeared. He was walking very slowly towards the group.

TORTOISE: I will race with you.

NARRATOR 2: The other animals stared at Tortoise. Then Hare burst out laughing.

HARE: You? You must be joking! You are so slow!

NARRATOR 1: The other animals laughed too. How could Tortoise ever beat Hare?

TORTOISE: I can beat you.

HARE: No, you can't.

TORTOISE: Yes, I can.

HARE: No, you can't.

TORTOISE: Yes, I can.

HARE: Well, I hate to see you make a fool of yourself, but OK.

TORTOISE: All right then. Let us begin.

8

NARRATOR 2: Hare turned toward the other animals.

HARE: Help us out, please.

MOUSE: On your marks . . .

NARRATOR 1: Tortoise and Hare lined up side by side.

SNAKE: Get sssssssset . . .

NARRATOR 2: Tortoise and Hare crouched down. They were ready to run!

FROG: Go!

CHEERING SQUAD 1: Go Tortoise!

CHEERING SQUAD 2: Go Hare!

NARRATOR 1: Tortoise started moving very slowly.

NARRATOR 2: Hare took off quickly, leaving Tortoise and the other animals behind. Horse looked at Tortoise.

HORSE: You have to move a little faster if you want to win.

TORTOISE: This is as fast as I go. Step by step, step by step.

NARRATOR 1: Hare was very far ahead by now. He decided to take a little nap.

HARE: That Tortoise will never catch up to me. When I wake up, I will make it to the finish line in plenty of time!

NARRATOR 2: Hare lay down and went to sleep.

NARRATOR 1: While Hare slept, Tortoise caught up with him. He kept going and slowly moved past Hare.

NARRATOR 2: The other animals saw this. They ran over to Hare and tried to wake him up.

MOUSE: Hare!

FROG: Wake up!

SNAKE: Tortoissssssse issssssss beating you!

NARRATOR 1: Hare stirred. Finally he was awake.

HARE: Huh? What? What is going on?

HORSE: Tortoise is ahead of you. Get going!

HARE: I have plenty of time! Please, let me nap!

NARRATOR 2: The other animals shrugged. Hare would not listen to them.

MOUSE: Fine. Rest then.

SNAKE: Let usssssss go catch up with Tortoisssssssse.

FROG: Hop to it!

HORSE: Giddy-yap!

NARRATOR 1: The animals ran to catch up with Tortoise. They watched as he crossed the finish line.

NARRATOR 2: Mouse patted Tortoise on his back.

MOUSE: Well done!

FROG: Great job!

SNAKE: Congratulationsssssss.

HORSE: Good going!

NARRATOR 1: Meanwhile, Hare had woken up. He looked at his watch and started off toward the finish line.

NARRATOR 2: Hare was out of breath when he caught up to the other animals. Then he saw that Tortoise had won the race. Hare spoke to Tortoise.

HARE: How did you beat me?

TORTOISE: Well, it is a little secret of mine.

HARE: Oh, come on. You can tell us.

SNAKE: Yesssssss, pleassssssse do.

FROG: What is the scoop?

MOUSE: We want to know.

HORSE: What is the secret?

TORTOISE: I learned this lesson from wise old Grandfather Tortoise: As you move from place to place, slow and steady wins the race.

HARE: How about another try? One more race. I know I can beat you this time.

TORTOISE: Maybe tomorrow. Right now I must go to the pond. A duck is waiting there for me. He wants to see who is the fastest swimmer.

MOUSE: May we come along?

TORTOISE: Of course.

NARRATOR 1: All the animals followed Tortoise, even Hare.

NARRATOR 2: As they walked they chanted the lesson Tortoise had just taught them.

ALL: As you move from place to place,
Slow and steady wins the race!

THE END

TEACHING GUIDE

READING THE PLAY

ABOUT "THE TORTOISE AND THE HARE"

"The Tortoise and the Hare" is known as an Aesop's fable. Many old stories are attributed to a storyteller named Aesop. Aesop was probably a legendary figure, but according to one source, he was an Ethiopian from Africa who lived as a slave in Greece more than 2,500 years ago. Aesop's owner eventually gave him his freedom. Under the rich King Croesus, Aesop acted as an ambassador in the Grecian provinces, telling stories to teach people to be good and honest. To avoid offending his listeners, he had animal characters act out the foolish ways of humans. His fables all contain moral lessons for listeners to think over. Some of Aesop's translators have made his lessons clearer by ending the stories with their moral. Other popular Aesop's fables include, "The Town Mouse and the Country Mouse" and "The Fox and the Crow."

QUESTIONS BEFORE READING THE PLAY

- What is the fastest animal you can think of? The slowest?
- A tortoise is a kind of turtle. What are turtles like?
- A hare is a kind of rabbit. What are rabbits like?
- Which do you think is faster, a tortoise or a hare?

WORDS TO PREVIEW

squad · scurry · gallop · slither · crouch · giddy-yap · steady

QUESTIONS AFTER READING THE PLAY

- Why didn't the other animals want to race with Hare?
- Why did the other animals laugh at Tortoise when he said he could beat Hare?
- Why did Hare take a nap during the race?
- Why do you think Tortoise won the race?
- What do you think "slow and steady wins the race" means?
- Do you think that telling stories is a good way to teach people a lesson?
- Can you think of any other stories that teach a lesson?

13

PERFORMING THE PLAY

⭐ Put desks in the center of the room. The Cheering Squads can watch the race from the center at their desks. Or place desks around the perimeter of the room with the Cheering Squads sitting on the floor in the center.

⭐ When Tortoise is about to finish the race, a student can jump up and hold a "FINISH" sign just in front of him or her to indicate the finish line.

WARM-UP EXERCISE

⭐ Have students pretend they are running very fast while standing in place. Then have them switch to a very slow pace. What changes? Is it only their feet? Do their arms change? How about their faces? Have students freeze in both fast and slow positions. Ask the class to comment on the differences.

EXTENSION ACTIVITIES

⭐ Ask students if they can recall a time when they have ever felt "left in the dust" by someone who was faster at something than they were (i.e. an older sibling). How did that make them feel? Then ask students to name some instances when going slower might actually be better than going fast. (Examples: eating ice cream, reading a book, paint-

ing a picture.) List students' ideas on the chalkboard to reinforce the idea that sometimes "slow and steady" really does win the race.

⭐ Make a mock newscast of the race between Tortoise and Hare. (You may ask students to watch a news program at home, or have them watch an afternoon broadcast as a class, to prepare for this activity.) Students can play different roles, such as news anchor, reporter, witnesses who saw the race, Tortoise, and Hare. The anchor person can start the activity by introducing the story. The reporter can then interview the various characters. Have remaining students ask the characters questions as in a news conference.

⭐ As a class, read other Aesop's fables to get a better feel for the genre. Then ask students to think of a moral lesson they feel is important, such as, "It is bad to cheat" or "Sharing is good." Have students write their own fables, teaching a lesson of their choice. Students can write and illustrate them as a class, in small groups, or individually. Compile all the fables into a book and refer to it if problems arise in class that are related to lessons taught in the book.

The Fisherman and His Wife

CHARACTERS

Narrator 1
Narrator 2
Fisherman
Fisherman's Wife
Fish

NARRATOR 1: Once upon a time there lived a fisherman and his wife. They lived in a hut by the sea.

NARRATOR 2: Their hut was small and they didn't have much money, but they were very happy.

FISHERMAN: Ah, my good wife. Smell that air! I am so happy here in our hut by the sea.

WIFE: Me, too, my husband. We have a roof over our heads and you always bring us fish to eat.

FISHERMAN: We are very lucky.

WIFE: Yes, we are.

NARRATOR 1: One day, like every other day, the fisherman was fishing in his little boat on the sea.

NARRATOR 2: Suddenly, he felt something tugging on his line. The tugging was so strong, he almost fell out of his boat.

FISHERMAN: Wow! That must be some fish!

NARRATOR 1: The fisherman pulled and pulled at his line, trying to get the fish out of the water.

NARRATOR 2: Finally, the fisherman pulled the fish out.

FISHERMAN: Wow! That is some fish indeed!

FISH: Why, yes, I am. Please, let me go.

FISHERMAN: Well, I can't do that because . . . hey, wait a minute, a talking fish?

FISH: I am not only a talking fish. I am a magic fish. I can give you anything you wish for.

FISHERMAN: That sounds a bit fishy if you ask me.

FISH: Maybe so, but it's true. What would you like? Let me go and your wish will come true.

FISHERMAN: Well, let me think. You know, I'm so happy with what I have, I can't think of a thing to wish for. But I will let you go anyway.

NARRATOR 1: The fisherman unhooked the fish from his line.

FISH: Thank you, kind sir. Bye-bye!

NARRATOR 2: And with that the fish swam away, deep down under the water.

NARRATOR 1: The fisherman hurried home. He couldn't wait to tell his wife what had happened.

FISHERMAN: Wife! Wife! The most amazing thing has happened!

WIFE: What is it, dear? Did you catch a lot of fish?

FISHERMAN: Well, no. I didn't catch any. But I met a talking fish, a magic fish. He said I could have anything I wished for.

WIFE: How wonderful! So, what did you ask this magic fish for?

FISHERMAN: Nothing. I told him I was happy with what I had.

WIFE: True, we are happy, but there must be something you could have wished for. What about a new house?

FISHERMAN: I thought you were happy in our hut.

WIFE: I am, but, a lovely cottage might make me happier. Won't you please go ask the fish for a lovely cottage?

FISHERMAN: If you wish.

NARRATOR 1: So the fisherman went back to the sea to ask the fish for a cottage.

NARRATOR 2: He stood in his boat and called out to the fish.

FISHERMAN: Yoo-hoo, magic fish!
        Come out of the sea!
        My wife has a wish,
        So she has sent me.

NARRATOR 1: The fish popped his head out of the water.

FISH: What is her wish, my friend?

FISHERMAN: She would like a lovely cottage.

FISH: So be it. Go home and you will find one.

NARRATOR 2: And the fish swam away, deep down under the water.

NARRATOR 1: The fisherman ran home to see if his wish had come true.

NARRATOR 2: He couldn't believe what he saw! His wife was sitting in front of a beautiful cottage.

WIFE: Welcome to our new home, my husband. Your fish has done a wonderful job!

FISHERMAN: That he has. The fish is very kind. Oh, we will be so happy in this cottage!

WIFE: Yes, but . . .

FISHERMAN: But what?

WIFE: This cottage is indeed lovely, but it's still a little small. I would like to live in a magnificent castle!

FISHERMAN: A castle? Whatever would we do with a castle?

WIFE: It would make me happier. Please, husband. Go and ask your fish friend for a magnificent castle.

FISHERMAN: If you wish.

NARRATOR 1: So the fisherman set off once again to find the fish.

NARRATOR 2: He rowed his boat to the middle of the sea and called for the fish.

FISHERMAN: Yoo-hoo, magic fish!
Come out of the sea!
My wife has a wish,
So she has sent me.

NARRATOR 1: The fish popped his head out of the water.

FISH: Another wish? Doesn't she like the cottage?

FISHERMAN: Oh, yes. The cottage is lovely. But now my wife wants a magnificent castle.

FISH: A castle? So be it. Go home and you will find one.

FISHERMAN: Oh thank you, dear fish! You are most kind.

NARRATOR 1: And the fish swam away, deep down under the water.

NARRATOR 2: The fisherman ran home. He wanted to see if his wish had come true. When he got home, his wife was standing in front of an enormous castle!

WIFE: Welcome to our new home, my husband. Isn't this a magnificent castle?

FISHERMAN: Yes, it is. The fish was very, very kind.

WIFE: Yes, he was. But . . .

FISHERMAN: But what?

WIFE: What good is living in a castle if you aren't king?

FISHERMAN: But I don't want to be king.

WIFE: Well, if you don't, I do! Go ask your fish friend to make me king!

FISHERMAN: But I have already asked him for too much. I can't ask him for more!

WIFE: Please, husband. Then I will be happy.

FISHERMAN: Well, all right. But this is the last time.

NARRATOR 1: So, the fisherman went to call upon the fish one more time.

FISHERMAN: Yoo-hoo, magic fish!
Come out of the sea!
My wife has a wish,
So she has sent me.

NARRATOR 2: The fish popped his head out of the water.

FISH: What could your wife possibly want now? Isn't the castle enough?

FISHERMAN: She loves the castle. But now she wants to be king.

FISH: King? Isn't she happy being a fisherman's wife?

FISHERMAN: I thought she was. But I guess she wants more now.

FISH: King, huh? Well, so be it. Go home and you will find one.

NARRATOR 1: And the fish swam away, deep down under the water. The fisherman hurried home. Was his wife really made king?

NARRATOR 2: As soon as the fisherman saw his wife, he knew that the answer was yes. She was sitting on a golden throne, wearing a beautiful jeweled crown.

FISHERMAN: My wife! Are you really king?

WIFE: I am. And you must call me "Your Majesty."

FISHERMAN: Yes, Your Majesty. And are you happy being king?

WIFE: Well, yes, but . . .

FISHERMAN: Don't tell me!

WIFE: Well, it's fine to rule over all of the people. But I want to be even more powerful. I want to rule over the sun and the moon!

FISHERMAN: Wife! I mean, Your Majesty, you can't be serious!

WIFE: I am. Go and ask your fish for what I wish.

FISHERMAN: I will not! You are not being fair!

WIFE: You will do as I say. I am your king!

FISHERMAN: Yes, Your Majesty.

NARRATOR 1: So the fisherman wearily called for the fish again.

FISHERMAN: Yoo-hoo, magic fish!
Come out of the sea!
My wife has a wish,
So she has sent me.

NARRATOR 2: The fish popped his head out of the water. He looked angry.

FISH: I don't believe it! Now what does she want?

FISHERMAN: My dear fish friend, I am so sorry to keep bothering you. My wife now wants to rule over the sun and the moon.

FISH: Enough is enough! Go home now. Your wife is back in her hut. She isn't a king anymore, only a fisherman's wife. That's what happens when you ask for too much.

NARRATOR 1: The fisherman hung his head. He was so ashamed.

FISH: Don't be sad. Remember how happy the two of you once were. Try to be happy again.

NARRATOR 2: The fisherman returned home. Many years passed. The fisherman and his wife were still living in their hut.

WIFE: Husband, it has been many years since you met the magic fish. Since then, nothing has changed. We live in the same hut by the sea. You go fishing every day. I keep our hut clean and prepare fine meals for us. And guess what?

FISHERMAN: What?

WIFE: I don't want anything else.

FISHERMAN: Nor do I, my wife. We have everything we need.

NARRATOR 1: So if you are ever down by the sea, look for a small hut.

NARRATOR 2: There you will find a very happy fisherman and his very happy wife.

THE END

TEACHING GUIDE

READING THE PLAY

ABOUT THE "THE FISHERMAN AND HIS WIFE"

"The Fisherman and His Wife" is a story in a famous collection of German folktales known as Grimm's Fairy Tales. The tales were collected by two brothers, Jacob and Wilhelm Grimm. The Grimms felt the tales expressed the spirit of the German people, and they published the tales to make sure they wouldn't be forgotten. Some of the Grimm brothers' most famous tales are "Hansel and Gretel," "Little Red Riding Hood," and "Snow White."

QUESTIONS BEFORE READING THE PLAY

- Have you ever wished for something? If so, what?
- Did you get what you wished for?
- What would you wish for if you could have anything?

WORDS TO PREVIEW

hut · cottage · magnificent · enormous · throne · majesty

QUESTIONS AFTER READING THE PLAY

- In what kind of place did the fisherman and his wife live at the beginning of the play?
- Did the fisherman wish for anything at first? Explain.
- What was the last thing the fisherman's wife asked for?
- Why do you think the fish got mad at the end of the play?

PERFORMING THE PLAY

⭐ The changing venues where the fisherman and his wife live can be represented very simply. A hut, cottage, and castle can be drawn on separate, large pieces of poster board. Two children can hold up each board while the particular scene is being enacted. To get more children involved, a different set of children can hold up each piece.

⭐ Other non-speaking parts that can be added to the play include fish swimming in the sea, servants working in the fisherman's cottage, and guards working in the castle.

WARM-UP EXERCISE

✻ Explain to students that many fish swim in schools, which move together in the same direction. Choose a volunteer to be the first leader. Then, with students standing in place, have the leader in front pretend that he or she is a fish swimming in a certain type of water, e.g., calm, rough, etc. The other students must follow the leader's movements, like fish in a school. Afterward, choose another leader to lead the group in a different type of water.

EXTENSION ACTIVITIES

✻ Ask students what is special about the way the fisherman calls for the fish. Then put four rhyming words on the board. Ask students what those words have in common. Have students write their own poems calling for the fish. Word combinations could include: fish, wish, swish, dish or sea, me, be, three. They can use the words in any order they choose. To extend the activity, incorporate the new poems when reading the play again.

✻ Invite students to pretend they are in a "School of Fish." Have them ponder questions such as: What kinds of things would fish have to learn? Who would be their teacher? Where would their lessons take place? Would there be any extra-curricular activities after school, such as sports or arts and crafts? After they answer those questions, have the class act out a "day in the fish school." Students can take turns playing the teacher, or the students can play different kinds of teachers, such as a swimming teacher, looking-for-food teacher, etc.

✻ Go on an imaginary deep-sea adventure with your students. Sit in a circle. Discuss what the class would need to go exploring underwater (e.g., mask, flippers, and oxygen). Then ask students to "suit up" and dive down into the water, while remaining seated. Ask them what they "see" underwater. When the exploration is completed, invite the class to draw what they saw. They can make individual drawings or, on a large piece of paper, the whole class can make a group underwater mural, with each student depicting on a piece of the mural what he or she "saw" on the journey.

The Little Red Hen

CHARACTERS

Ma Jones
Pa Jones
Hen
Duck
Cat
Dog
Sheep
Pig
Cow

MA JONES: Boy! Planting this wheat sure is a lot of work!

PA JONES: You're right. I'm glad we're working together. This would be a hard job to do alone.

MA JONES: But our little red hen did it alone, remember?

PA JONES: Yep. She was some gal. It seems like just yesterday she was scratching in the farmyard. It was time for planting wheat. The little red hen wanted some help.

HEN: Oh, what a lovely day. It is the perfect time for planting wheat. Who will plant with me?

DUCK: Not I.

MA JONES: Said the duck.

CAT: Not I.

PA JONES: Said the cat.

DOG: Not I.

MA JONES: Said the dog.

SHEEP: Not I.

PA JONES: Said the sheep.

PIG: Not I.

MA JONES: Said the pig.

COW: Not I.

PA JONES: Said the cow.

HEN: Very well, then. I will plant it myself.

MA JONES: So she planted the wheat all by herself. After a while the wheat grew tall. It was ready to be cut.

HEN: The wheat has grown very tall indeed. I sure could use some help cutting it. Who will help me?

DUCK: Not I.

PA JONES: Said the duck.

CAT: Not I.

MA JONES: Said the cat.

DOG: Not I.

PA JONES: Said the dog.

SHEEP: Not I.

MA JONES: Said the sheep.

PIG: Not I.

PA JONES: Said the pig.

COW: Not I.

MA JONES: Said the cow.

HEN: Very well, then. I will cut it myself.

PA JONES: So the hen cut the wheat all by herself. Then it was time for the wheat to be threshed. The little red hen called upon her friends again.

HEN: There is much wheat here to be threshed. Who will help me?

DUCK: Not I.

MA JONES: Said the duck.

CAT: Not I.

PA JONES: Said the cat.

DOG: Not I.

MA JONES: Said the dog.

SHEEP: Not I.

PA JONES: Said the sheep.

PIG: Not I.

MA JONES: Said the pig.

COW: Not I.

PA JONES: Said the cow.

HEN: Very well, then. I will thresh it myself.

MA JONES: So the little red hen threshed the wheat all by herself. Then it was time to bring it to the mill to be ground into flour.

PA JONES: She wouldn't give up, would she? She asked her friends for help once again.

HEN: This wheat is ready to be taken to the mill to be ground into flour. Who will help me?

DUCK: Not I.

MA JONES: Said the duck.

CAT: Not I.

PA JONES: Said the cat.

DOG: Not I.

MA JONES: Said the dog.

SHEEP: Not I.

PA JONES: Said the sheep.

PIG: Not I.

MA JONES: Said the pig.

COW: Not I.

PA JONES: Said the cow.

HEN: Very well, then. I will bring it to the mill myself.

MA JONES: And she did. When the wheat was all ground up into flour, it was time to make bread.

PA JONES: I remember what happened next. She went to those so-called friends of hers.

HEN: Time to use this flour to make some tasty loaves of bread! Who will help me?

DUCK: Not I.

MA JONES: Said the duck.

CAT: Not I.

PA JONES: Said the cat.

DOG: Not I.

MA JONES: Said the dog.

SHEEP: Not I.

PA JONES: Said the sheep.

PIG: Not I.

MA JONES: Said the pig.

COW: Not I.

PA JONES: Said the cow.

HEN: Very well, then. I will bake the bread myself.

MA JONES: And she did. And boy, oh boy, did that fresh bread smell good!

PA JONES: I could smell it baking clear across the fields. Mmmmm, mmmmm!

MA JONES: But here's the best part. After all the bread was baked, you know what time it was?

PA JONES: Eating time! Those friends wanted to help out with that, huh?

MA JONES: They sure did. But she was smart.

HEN: Look at all that wonderful bread! It is time to eat it. Who will eat with me?

DUCK: I will!

PA JONES: Said the duck.

CAT: I will!

MA JONES: Said the cat.

DOG: I will!

PA JONES: Said the dog.

SHEEP: I will!

MA JONES: Said the sheep.

PIG: I will!

PA JONES: Said the pig.

COW: I will!

MA JONES: Said the cow.

HEN: Oh, no you won't. None of you helped me before. This is one job I can handle all by myself. Gladly!

MA AND PA JONES: And that little red hen of ours ate and ate until she was nice and full.

THE END

TEACHING GUIDE

READING THE PLAY

ABOUT "THE LITTLE RED HEN"
"The Little Red Hen" is an old English tale. Like many other fairy tales, it is a moralistic story that tells of the rewards of industriousness over laziness. "The Little Red Hen" is an empowering story that shows that with determination and effort, great tasks can be accomplished.

QUESTIONS BEFORE READING THE PLAY
- Do you have any chores at home or in your classroom? If so, what are they?
- Has anyone ever helped you with your chores? If so, did this make the chores easier or harder?
- If people don't help with work, should they be rewarded? Why or why not?
- Do you know how bread is made?

WORDS TO PREVIEW
wheat · thresh · mill · flour

QUESTIONS AFTER READING THE PLAY
- What did the little red hen want from the other animals? Did she get what she wanted?
- Why wouldn't the little red hen let the other animals eat the bread she made? Do you think she was right or wrong?
- What do you think might happen the next time the little red hen asks for help?

PERFORMING THE PLAY

✧ The farmers should remain on the stage throughout the play. They can be in front of, behind, or alongside the playing area where the animal action is taking place.

✧ To include more students, animal parts can be added. These additional animals would simply say the same line ("Not I.") as the others. The farmers would then say "Said the _____" inserting whichever animal has been added. Some suggestions for additional animal parts are: goose, goat, horse, mouse, and donkey.

WARM-UP EXERCISE

- To accustom students to the rhythmic language in the play and the echo-like response incorporated in it, try this activity: Ask your class to sit in a circle. Start a rhythm going by having everyone pat their laps twice, then clap their hands, then hold for a beat. Example: pat, pat, clap, hold, pat, pat, clap, hold. Go around the circle and have each child say his or her name to the beat: My name is Nick. Then, keeping with the beat, have the rest of the class respond with, "Hello, Nick!" and continue around the circle until each child has said his or her name.

EXTENSION ACTIVITIES

- Ask students to pick their favorite character in the play. Have them draw a picture of that character. Younger children can then write a short caption under their character's picture. For example, if a child chooses the duck, he or she can write, "'Not I,' said the duck." Encourage older children to write a short story about their character under the picture, (e.g., a story about why the cow didn't feel like helping that day.)

- Ask students to pretend that they are members of the farm community portrayed in the play. Hold a farm meeting about the lack of cooperation in getting chores done. The problem should be discussed and decisions made as to how to solve it. If some course of action is proposed, to extend the activity, role-play a situation in which that solution is implemented. Does it achieve the desired results?

- To help your students become more familiar with where different foods come from, read some "farm-to-table" process books together. Some favorites of mine are:

  - From Grain to Bread by Ali Mitgutsch (Carolrhoda Books, 1981). Child-friendly illustrations lead children through the bread-making process, from the growing of wheat on a farm to the baking of pretzels and loaves of bread. This book is one in a series from Carolrholda called From Start to Finish. Other titles in this series include From Blossom to Honey, From Milk to Ice Cream, and From Seed to Pear.

  - Make Me a Peanut Butter Sandwich and a Glass of Milk by Ken Robbins (Scholastic, 1992). This photo essay shows all that goes into producing this favorite snack, taking readers from peanut plant to peanut butter, wheat to bread, and cow to milk, with simple language and lush photographs.

The Bremen Town Musicians

CHARACTERS

Narrator 1 Y Me
Narrator 2
Donkey — Kevin
Dog — Bobby
Cat — Aaron
Rooster — Chris
Robber 1 — Josh
Robber 2 — Mitchell
Robber 3 — Dominiah

NARRATOR 1: Once there was a donkey. He worked hard for his owner for many years. Day after day he carried heavy bags of grain to the mill.

NARRATOR 2: But the donkey grew old. He could no longer work hard. One day he heard his owner talking about him. He said he was going to get rid of the donkey. The donkey was worried.

DONKEY: Oh, no! What will happen to me? I must run away. I'll go to Bremen. There I can be a fine musician.

The donkey sings this song:

> Off I go to Bremen Town.
> It's the place to be!

I will play my music there.
People will love me!
With a hee-haw here, and a hee-haw there,
Here a hee, there a haw,
Everywhere a hee-haw.
Off I go to Bremen Town.
It's the place to be!

NARRATOR 1: So the donkey left that night. He had not gone far when he saw a dog lying on the ground.

NARRATOR 2: The dog looked weak. He also looked sad. The donkey knelt down to speak to the dog.

DONKEY: What is the matter, my friend?

DOG: Ah, me. Now that I am old and weak, I can no longer hunt. My owner wants to get rid of me. I got scared, so I ran away. Now I don't know what I will do.

DONKEY: You can come with me to Bremen. I am going to be a musician. Will you join me?

DOG: I'd love to! I can bark very pleasant tunes.

DOG AND DONKEY: Off we go to Bremen Town.
It's the place to be!
We will play our music there.
We'll be filled with glee!

DONKEY: With a hee-haw here, and a hee-haw there,
Here a hee, there a haw, everywhere a hee-haw.

DOG: With a bow-wow here and a bow-wow there
Here a bow, there a wow, everywhere a bow-wow.

DOG AND DONKEY: Off we go to Bremen Town.
It's the place to be!

NARRATOR 1: So, the donkey and the dog set off for Bremen. Soon, they saw a cat sitting by the road.

NARRATOR 2: The cat had the saddest face the donkey and the dog had ever seen. They stopped to find out what was wrong.

DOG: Hello there. Why so glum?

CAT: Ho, hum. Now that I am old and my teeth are not sharp, I cannot catch mice. My owner wants to get rid of me. I don't know what I will do.

DONKEY: You'll come to Bremen with us, that's what! We are going to become musicians. Won't you join us?

CAT: Sure I will! I love to meow.

DONKEY, DOG, AND CAT: Off we go to Bremen Town.
It's the place to be!
We will play our music there.
We're a gifted three!

DONKEY: With a hee-haw here, and a hee-haw there.
Here a hee, there a haw, everywhere a hee-haw.

DOG: With a bow-wow here, and a bow-wow there.
Here a bow, there a wow, everywhere a bow-wow.

CAT: With a meow-meow here, and a meow-meow there.
Here a meow, there a meow, everywhere a meow-meow.

ALL: Off we go to Bremen Town.
It's the place to be!

NARRATOR 1: The three musicians walked along some more. They came to a farmyard. There they heard a rooster crowing sadly.

ROOSTER: Cock-a-doodle-doo! Cock-a-doodle-doo!

DONKEY: My, you sound so sad. What is wrong?

ROOSTER: I used to crow to wake up the farmer each morning. But he just bought an alarm clock. Now he doesn't need my crowing so he wants to get rid of me. Now I'm a cock-a-doodle-don't! Oh, what will I do?

DOG: Come with us to Bremen. We're going to be musicians.

CAT: With your fine crowing, we'll make a wonderful group!

ROOSTER: I cock-a-doodle-<u>do</u> think that's a wonderful idea! Let's go!

DONKEY, DOG, CAT, AND ROOSTER:
>Off we go to Bremen Town.
>It's the place to be!
>We will play our music there.
>We're a sight to see!

DONKEY: With a hee-haw here, and a hee-haw there.
>Here a hee, there a haw, everywhere a hee-haw.

DOG: With a bow-wow here, and a bow-wow there.
>Here a bow, there a wow, everywhere a bow-wow.

CAT: With a meow-meow here, and a meow-meow there.
>Here a meow, there a meow, everywhere a meow-meow.

ROOSTER: With a cock-a-doodle here, and a cock-a-doodle there.
>Here a doodle, there a doodle, everywhere a cock-a-doodle.

ALL: Off we go to Bremen Town.
It's the place to be!

NARRATOR 2: The four musicians walked until it got dark. Finally they saw a sign that said Bremen Town. They danced with excitement but they were also very tired. They wanted to rest.

NARRATOR 1: They saw light coming from a little house up the road. They walked up to the window, but none of the animals were tall enough to see inside. So, the dog stood on the donkey's back, the cat stood on the dog's back, and the rooster stood on the cat's back and peeked inside.

DOG: What do you see, rooster?

DONKEY: I think there are three robbers in there! They are sitting at a table full of delicious-looking food!

CAT: Food? I'm starving! What shall we do? We must get them out of that house!

ROOSTER: I have a plan. Listen closely.

NARRATOR 2: The rooster whispered his plan to the others.

NARRATOR 1: All of a sudden, the four began singing. They made quite a noise. When the robbers heard the animals, they ran out of the house screaming!

NARRATOR 2: The four musicians went inside the house. There they ate and ate until they were full. Then, it was time for bed.

NARRATOR 1: The donkey slept in the soft grass in the yard. The dog slept behind the front door. The cat slept near the warmth of the fireplace. And the rooster slept high on a book shelf.

NARRATOR 2: After a while, the robbers returned to finish eating their feast.

ROBBER 1: That noise was probably just the wind. Besides, I can't wait to eat the rest of that roast beef!

ROBBER 2: I can taste those mashed potatoes now!

ROBBER 3: I'll go first just to make sure it's safe.

NARRATOR 1: So the robber went inside. He was cold, so he went to the fireplace to warm himself. There he surprised the cat, who scratched his face.

NARRATOR 2: The robber ran to the front door. The dog was startled and bit his leg. The robber ran outside. He tripped over the donkey, who kicked him.

NARRATOR 1: All this noise woke the rooster up. He started screeching, "Cock-a-doodle-doo!" The robber ran back to his friends.

ROBBER 3: There are four horrible monsters in there! One scratched me with its long nails. Another bit me. Another kicked me. And the fourth one screamed, "Coming to get yooouuuuu!"

ROBBER 1: Four monsters! Let's get out of here!

NARRATOR 2: And the robbers ran off, never to be heard from again.

NARRATOR 1: But the four musicians stayed there. They sang every night in Bremen, where they became the famous Bremen Town Musicians!

THE END

TEACHING GUIDE

READING THE PLAY

ABOUT "THE BREMEN TOWN MUSICIANS"

"The Bremen Town Musicians" is another tale by the Brothers Grimm. It tells the story of four unwanted animals who succeed, through determination, effort, and teamwork.

Bremen is a city in Germany. Visitors to the city today can see a statue of the four musicians, built in honor of their story.

QUESTIONS BEFORE READING THE PLAY

- What do you think teamwork means?
- Do you like working in a group?
- Do you think there are good things about working in a group? What are they?

WORDS TO PREVIEW

grain · mill · musician · pleasant · tunes · glum · gifted

QUESTIONS AFTER READING THE PLAY

- Why did the animals want to run away?
- Why did they decide to go to Bremen?
- How did they scare the robbers away?
- Do you think teamwork always help people succeed? Are there things you prefer to do by yourself? What are some things you do that benefit from teamwork?

PERFORMING THE PLAY

✫ Have the anamals sing the song "Off I go to Bremen Town" to the tune of "Old MacDonald Had a Farm."

✫ The journey the animals take to Bremen lends itself nicely to an in-the-round production. Each animal can be in place as the play opens. Then, one by one, the group grows as a new animal is added to the group, which makes its way around the classroom. The donkey can start by walking around one part of the classroom, where he meets up with the dog. Then those two continue around the classroom and they meet up with the cat, etc.

✫ The scene where the animals stand on top of one another to see into the house can be challenging. Since it is unreason-

able to actually stand the children on top of one another, you'll have to "cheat" the pyramid effect. For example, have the donkey crouch, and the dog stand on tiptoes behind the donkey. The cat can stand on a book or something raised behind the cat, and the rooster on something a bit higher than the cat.

WARM-UP EXERCISE

To get the feeling of teamwork across to your students, invite them to become a human machine. First, ask each student to come up with a movement and a sound for their part of an imaginary machine. Ask each child to demonstrate their movement and sound to the class. Then have them gather together—they should either be touching each other, or simply standing close to each other to get the feeling that they are all part of one machine. On the count of three, have all the students perform their movement and sound together. Afterward, ask students what kind of machine they were and what the machine's function was. How did each individual part contribute to that function?

EXTENSION ACTIVITIES

Explain the concept of strategy to your class. A strategy is a plan people come up with in order to achieve a certain result. The rooster's strategy for seeing inside the house was to have the animals stand on top of one another. Show stu-

dents how they use strategies every day to solve problems. For example, if they have to reach something high up, how might they do it? One option would be to stand on something. Another would be to ask someone tall to get it for them. Ask each child to come up with something they would like to achieve and develop a strategy for doing so. Have students share their ideas with the class. Have the class suggest strategies that each student could use to achieve his or her goal. At the end of the exercise, see if there are common elements in the strategies, such as "work hard" or "don't give up." Write these ideas on a piece of poster board and hang it in your classroom for your students to refer to when they need help with problem solving.

Use the play to devise math questions to teach or reinforce addition and subtraction. Start with the donkey. Ask how many animals there were in the beginning of the play, then how many when the donkey met the dog, when the donkey and the dog met the cat, and so on. After you have discussed these equations, invite children to develop word problems based on the play.

41

The Little Red Lighthouse and the Great Gray Bridge

CHARACTERS

Narrator 1
Narrator 2
Little Red Lighthouse
Steamship
Canoe
Tug Boat
Lighthouse Keeper
Bridge Builder 1
Bridge Builder 2
Great Gray Bridge

NARRATOR 1:
> There once was a lighthouse whose bright, shining beam
> Was the lightest and brightest folks had ever seen.

NARRATOR 2:
> He was faded and rusty and not very tall,
> But that didn't bother the lighthouse at all.

LIGHTHOUSE:
> To warn boats of danger, I ring my bell loud.
> I am quite important! I am very proud!

NARRATOR 1:
> Each morning the lighthouse's friends would appear.
> Sometimes they whistled. Sometimes they cheered.

STEAMSHIP: Well, hooty-toot-toot! And a how do you do?

NARRATOR 2: Said the big steamship from the water so blue.

CANOE: Well, hello my friend! What a day for a glide!

NARRATOR 1: Said the slender canoe taking folks for a ride.

TUGBOAT: Chug, chug, chug, and cheerio!

NARRATOR 2: Said the tug who had quite a long way to go.

NARRATOR 1:
> When night came the lighthouse keeper arrived
> To make the now quiet lighthouse come alive.

LIGHTHOUSE KEEPER:
> It's my job to keep the lighthouse shining bright
> So he can warn ships in the darkness of night.

NARRATOR 2:
> The lighthouse then flashed his bright beam of light.
> He rang his bell with all of his might.

LIGHTHOUSE:
> Watch out for the rocks! Please keep away!
> Watch me closely, so safe you'll stay!

NARRATOR 1:
> One day some workers came to dig
> In the river which was so big.

NARRATOR 2:

> They planted steel beams in the river floor.
> They rested a bit, then they planted some more.

NARRATOR 1:

> The beams stretched up high and before they were through,
> The steel beams were crossing the water so blue!

BRIDGE BUILDER 1: We build beams over the river wide.

BRIDGE BUILDER 2: So people can reach the other side.

LIGHTHOUSE:

> What is this strange new sight?
> Somehow I don't feel quite right.

NARRATOR 2:

> The workers stopped building late one day.
> And there stood a bridge that was big and gray.

LIGHTHOUSE:

> That big gray bridge sure is tall!
> But now I feel incredibly small.

NARRATOR 1:

> Then the bridge gave off a beam of light,
> and the lighthouse felt a terrible fright.

LIGHTHOUSE:

> Oh no! She is much brighter than me!
> She is much easier for boats to see!
> I don't feel needed anymore.
> The bridge can guide the boats to shore.

NARRATOR 2:

> The lighthouse sniffled. Then he cried.
> He felt so very sad inside.

44

NARRATOR 1:

When night came, the lighthouse began to fret.
The lighthouse keeper had not come yet.

LIGHTHOUSE:

Without my lighthouse-keeper friend,
My fun job has come to an end.
I guess the keeper stayed at home
Because the bridge can do it alone.

NARRATOR 2:

Just then the wind began to blow.
It tossed the tug boat to and fro.

TUG:

Oh, where is the lighthouse's shining light?
I need it to guide me on this stormy night.

NARRATOR 1:

Just when the tug thought he had reached the docks,
CRASH! He went tumbling against the rocks!

NARRATOR 2:

The bridge saw this and she began to shout
Down to the lighthouse whose light was still out.

BRIDGE:

Hello there, my friend. Why don't you blink?
Without your beam, the ships will sink.

LIGHTHOUSE:

But I thought that your light was enough
To guide the boats when the water is rough.

BRIDGE:

I shine for airplanes, the boats of the sky.
Your light shines down low and my light shines up high.

NARRATOR 1:
>Just then the lighthouse keeper appeared.
>When the lighthouse saw him he let out a cheer.

LIGHTHOUSE:
>Where have you been? You gave me a scare.
>I could not tell the boats to beware.

LIGHTHOUSE KEEPER:
>I lost my keys, but now they're found.
>We sure missed your light and sound.

BRIDGE:
>You see, my friend. Please have no doubt.
>Your light is something boats can't do without.

TUG:
>That is for sure. You're telling me!
>If your light had shone I'd have been able to see.

NARRATOR 1: Just then the steamship and canoe came by.

NARRATOR 2: They wanted to cheer up that sad little guy.

STEAMSHIP: You are our lighthouse. You are our friend.

CANOE: We never want your job to end.

LIGHTHOUSE:
>So, even though I'm short and small,
>I am still needed after all.

ALL: Yes, you are still needed after all!

THE END

46

TEACHING GUIDE

READING THE PLAY

ABOUT "THE LITTLE RED LIGHTHOUSE AND THE GREAT GRAY BRIDGE"

"The Little Red Lighthouse and the Great Gray Bridge" is the story of an actual lighthouse that stands beneath the George Washington Bridge on the Hudson River in New York City. The lighthouse was built in 1921 and was made famous by a children's tale written by Hildegarde H. Swift and Lynd Ward. The story tells of a lighthouse who realizes that even though he is small, he is very much needed by the ships who sail up and down the Hudson. The story helps children realize that everyone has unique qualities that make him or her special and necessary.

QUESTIONS BEFORE READING THE PLAY

- Do you know what a lighthouse is?
- What is a lighthouse's job? How does it do its job?
- What do you think might happen if there were no lighthouses?

WORDS TO PREVIEW

beam · steamship · canoe · tug · glide · cheerio · steel · beams · incredibly · guide · docks

QUESTIONS AFTER READING THE PLAY

- Why was lighthouse sad about the bridge?
- Why do people build bridges?
- Why was the Little Red Lighthouse happy at the end of the play?

PERFORMING THE PLAY

✮ You may want to have two students play the bridge. They can make a bridge formation as is done when playing "London Bridge is Falling Down." If you play the bridge in this way, the children acting as the bridge can take turns saying the bridge's lines.

WARM-UP EXERCISE

✷ As a class, come up with a pose for a lighthouse and a pose for a bridge. For example, students may form lighthouses by making their arms in a point above their head. They may become bridges by bending at the waist and extending their arms out as though reaching across a body of water. Then, play a game of "Simon Says" using only the words "lighthouse" and "bridge." For example, the leader will say, "Simon says Lighthouse," and the children go into their lighthouse pose. This warm-up will give all students the chance to feel like a lighthouse and a bridge whether they are playing the parts in the play or not.

EXTENSION ACTIVITIES

✷ When your students have a clear idea of the purposes that lighthouses and bridges serve, try this geography/art activity: Make copies of any kind of map containing land masses, bodies of water, and rocky shoals or sandbars. Ask students to draw a lighthouse wherever they think one might come in handy. Then ask them to do the same for a bridge. Invite them to share their maps with the class and to explain why they placed the lighthouse and the bridge where they did.

✷ Both the lighthouse and the bridge have lights used for safety. The lighthouse light keeps boats safe and the bridge light keeps airplanes safe. Invite your class to think about other kinds of safety lights. (Some examples are traffic lights and lights on bicycles.) Ask them how these lights keep people safe. Make a "Lights On for Safety" chart listing the different types of lights on one side and the safety purposes they serve on the other. You may want to extend the activity by taking a mini-field trip around your school and seeing how many safety lights the class can find.

The Nightingale

CHARACTERS

Mother Bird
Little Bird 1
Little Bird 2
Nightingale
Emperor
Servant 1
Servant 2
Cow
Frog
Toy Bird

MOTHER BIRD: Gather around, children. I want to tell you a story.

LITTLE BIRD 1: What is the story about, mother?

MOTHER BIRD: It is about your great-great grandmother nightingale.

LITTLE BIRD 2: The one who lived in China?

LITTLE BIRD 1: And sang so sweetly?

MOTHER BIRD: That is her.

LITTLE BIRD 1 AND 2: Oh, tell us!

MOTHER BIRD: Well, long ago, in a far-off land called China, deep in the forest, there lived a nightingale.

LITTLE BIRD 2: Our great-great grandma!

MOTHER BIRD: That's right. She sang so beautifully that even the fish in the sea would stop swimming to listen to her sing.

NIGHTINGALE: Tra-la-la! Tra-la-lee! La-la-tra-la-lee!

MOTHER BIRD: One day, the Emperor of China was walking in his garden when he heard the nightingale singing.

NIGHTINGALE: La-la-tra-la! Tra-la-la! Tra-la-tra-la-lee!

EMPEROR: Who is that singing? That is the most beautiful singing I have ever heard! Servants, come here at once!

SERVANT 1: Yes, mighty Emperor?

SERVANT 2: What can we do for you?

EMPEROR: Do you hear that singing?

NIGHTINGALE: Tra-la-la! Tra-la-lee!

SERVANT 1: Oh yes.

SERVANT 2: It's lovely!

EMPEROR: Well, I must have it! Please, go find whoever is singing and bring him or her to me. Whoever it is must dine with me this evening.

MOTHER BIRD: So the servants went off into the forest to try to find the singer. On the way they heard a sound.

COW: Moo! Moo!

SERVANT 1: Oh! There it is! That's the singer!

SERVANT 2: Don't be silly! That's a cow!

COW: Moo! Moo!

SERVANT 1: Oops! You're right. Let's keep going.

MOTHER BIRD: So the two walked deeper into the forest. Then they heard another sound.

FROG: Ribbit! Ribbit!

SERVANT 1: Listen! What a beautiful song. Let's bring the singer to the Emperor.

SERVANT 2: Listen more closely, my friend. That's a frog croaking!

FROG: Ribbit! Ribbit!

SERVANT 2: Ooops! You're right. Let's keep going.

MOTHER BIRD: And the two walked deeper still into the forest. Suddenly they stopped in their tracks, for they heard the beautiful singing of the nightingale.

NIGHTINGALE: Tra-la-lee! Tra-la-la!

SERVANT 1: There she is!

SERVANT 2: That small gray bird? Ha! I don't believe it! I expected someone much more beautiful and fancy.

SERVANT 1: Miss Nightingale, our Emperor loves your singing. He would like you to join him for dinner this evening.

NIGHTINGALE: It would be my pleasure! Tra-la-la!

MOTHER BIRD: So the servants and the nightingale went to the Emperor's palace.

LITTLE BIRD 1: Was the palace beautiful, Mother?

MOTHER BIRD: Oh yes, very. Everything was covered in gold and jewels. The Emperor had set up a golden perch for the nightingale to sit on. Many people came to hear the nightingale's song.

EMPEROR: My dear nightingale, please sing for us.

NIGHTINGALE: Tra-la-la! Tra-la-lee! Tra-la-la! Tra-la-lee!

LITTLE BIRD 2: And did the Emperor enjoy the song?

MOTHER BIRD: He liked it so much, he smiled the biggest smile anyone had ever seen!

EMPEROR: Nightingale, your song makes me so happy. I would like you to live here in the palace. Then I can hear your singing all the time.

LITTLE BIRD 1: What a lucky bird! She got to live in the beautiful palace.

MOTHER BIRD: Well, the nightingale was not so happy. She was kept in a cage that was guarded at all times.

NIGHTINGALE: It makes me happy to see the Emperor smile, but I miss my home in the forest.

MOTHER BIRD: One day, the Emperor got a present. Inside a golden box was a toy bird. The bird was gold and covered with diamonds. He was the most beautiful thing the Emperor had ever seen.

EMPEROR: Listen! When I wind up this toy bird, he sings a beautiful song.

TOY BIRD: La-la-la! La-la-la!

MOTHER BIRD: Everyone gathered around to hear the toy bird's song. While they weren't paying attention to her, the nightingale opened up the gate to her cage and flew out the window and back to the forest.

SERVANT 2: The nightingale has flown away!

EMPEROR: That's OK. I now have this new bird. He sings just as sweetly and is much more beautiful!

SERVANT 1: But Emperor, this bird keeps singing the same song over and over. The nightingale sang many different songs.

TOY BIRD: La-la-la! La-la-la!

EMPEROR: Quiet! It's a perfectly good song. Who needs different songs?

MOTHER BIRD: The Emperor set the toy bird on a velvet pillow. Whenever the Emperor wanted to hear a song, he would wind up the toy bird and it would sing.

TOY BIRD: La-la-la!

MOTHER BIRD: After a year, though, the toy bird broke. He could not sing anymore. The palace became very quiet. Then the Emperor became very sick. He lay in his bed all the time.

EMPEROR: Music would make me feel much better. Hey! Toy bird! Sing for me!

MOTHER BIRD: But the toy bird just sat and stared straight ahead. All of a sudden, the Emperor heard singing outside his window. He pulled back the curtains and there was the nightingale!

NIGHTINGALE: Tra-la-la! Tra-la-lee!

EMPEROR: Nightingale! You have returned! Oh, how I missed your song! You gave me so much and I treated you so badly. How can I ever repay you?

NIGHTINGALE: Your smile when I sing is my reward. Tra-la-la!

EMPEROR: You must stay with me always. Already I feel myself getting better.

NIGHTINGALE: No. My home is in the forest. But I will come to you often. In the evening I will sit by your window and sing for you. But you must promise me one thing.

EMPEROR: Yes. Anything.

NIGHTINGALE: Promise me this will be our secret. I will sing only for you.

MOTHER BIRD: So the Emperor promised. And the nightingale sang. And the Emperor got well and nobody ever knew that music was the medicine that cured him.

THE END

TEACHING GUIDE

READING THE PLAY

ABOUT "THE NIGHTINGALE"
The author of this tale is Hans Christian Andersen, the famous nineteenth-century Danish writer. Andersen's fairy tales are among the most widely read works in the world. He wrote 168 tales. Some of his most popular stories are "The Ugly Duckling," "The Emperor's New Clothes," "Thumbelina," "The Little Mermaid," and "The Nightingale."

As is true of many fairy tales, a number of Andersen's stories have serious moral meanings intended for adult readers. But the story of "The Nightingale" and its message of appreciating—and treating well—those you love is a valuable lesson to readers of all ages.

QUESTIONS BEFORE READING THE PLAY
- Do you know what a nightingale is?
- Have you ever heard birds singing? How did their sounds make you feel?
- Would you rather have a real live bird or a toy bird? Why?

WORDS TO PREVIEW
servants · Emperor · mighty · perch · velvet · reward · cured

QUESTIONS AFTER READING THE PLAY
- Why did the Emperor want the nightingale to live with him?
- Why did the nightingale run away?
- What did the Emperor like about the toy bird?
- What happened to the toy bird?
- Why do you think the nightingale wanted to be kept a secret at the end of the play?

PERFORMING THE PLAY

✫ To create the space where the bird family lives, set aside an area apart from the main playing space. You may want to place the family in a nestlike setting. To do this, you can place blankets or towels in a little bunch and have the bird family nestle there. Place sticks around the blankets to make the blanketed area look more like a nest.

✫ To get more children involved, cast more than one cow and frog.

✫ Costuming for the toy bird can be as ornate or as simple as your resources allow. If you don't have costume jewelry, simply wrap part of the child playing that part in aluminum foil to give the illusion of a sparkly, artificial bird.

WARM-UP EXERCISE

✭ To show how sound can express different emotions, try this exercise: Choose a string of syllables to use—for example, la-la-la. Ask students to sing or simply say the syllables together. As they do so, call out different emotions like sad, mad, happy, etc., and ask them to imagine and show these emotions while singing. Ask them to pay attention to how the different facial expressions they show with each emotion change the sounds of the words.

EXTENSION ACTIVITIES

✭ Ask students to construct a Venn diagram showing the similarities and differences between the nightingale and the toy bird. In one circle, have children write qualities possessed only by the nightingale, e.g., the color gray. In the other circle, ask children to write characteristics of the toy bird, e.g., jeweled. In the center, where the circles share a space, have children write the characteristics that the two birds have in common, e.g., they both sing. Do the birds have more commonalities or differences? Which bird do they prefer? Why?

✭ To experience different bird songs, try going on a nature walk around your school grounds. Ask students to try to imitate the different bird songs they hear. Even if your school is in the city, sparrows and pigeons can most likely be found, and these two birds make very distinct sounds. Try using a bird guide to identify the birds you find.

✭ As a class, write a song for the nightingale. You may want to write the words first and make up a tune to fit them later. Or simply write nightingale-appropriate lyrics to go with a familiar tune, such as "Row, Row, Row Your Boat." The song can be about the story in the play or it can be extended to include other aspects of the nightingale's life. If your students perform the play, you might wish to incorporate the new nightingale song into the script.